Table of Contents

Preface

The basis for drafting this paper was an attempt to understand the root causes of violence against Americans, specifically by those who use Islam as their justification. The hope is that better understanding of this challenge can lead to shaping better U.S. foreign policies. In developing this argument I would like to acknowledge the mentorship provided by Dr. John P. Cann, PhD, and LtCol John R. Wilkerson. Equally welcome was the wisdom and insight offered by Peter J. and Susan C. Boone.

Radical Islam

Introduction

And the angel of the Lord said unto her, Behold, thou art with child, and shalt bear a son, and shalt call his name Ishmael; because the Lord hath heard thy affliction. And he will be a wild man; his hand will be against every man, and every man's hand against him; and he shall dwell in the presence of all his brethren.

-The Angel of the Lord to Hagar, Genesis 16:11-12

Abraham is widely regarded as the father of Islam, Christianity and Judaism. Ishmael, his son by Hagar, an Egyptian slave, is the first genealogical and chronological point where Islam deviates from its monotheistic antecedents. That much, and often less, is generally known in the West about a religion that claims Judeo-Christian roots. That Islam is inscrutable to the average Westerner is obvious. Until recently, Western societies seem to have managed well for almost 1,400 years without a proper understanding of a religion claimed today by over 1 billion souls. What has made Islam a household word and frequent thought, if not fear, is its apparent proclivity to violence. The relevance of the subject is central today given recent terrorist attacks stemming from this source and culminating in the September 11th, 2001, attacks on the World Trade Center and the Pentagon. However, assuming that this threat is dismissed with the elimination of Osama bin Laden or any other terrorist is a mistake.[1] This paper seeks to give the reader a more comprehensive understanding of radical Islam and the consequences it will have for contemporary policy-makers by tracing its roots from the 7th century AD and evaluating its course to the present.

---

[1] The use of the word *Terrorist* is curtailed in this paper, largely owing to the complications of arriving at a suitable definition.

The Character of Islam

Those who believe fight in the way of Allah, and those who disbelieve fight in the

way of the Shaitan. Fight therefore against the friends of the Shaitan; surely the

strategy of the Shaitan is weak.

-The Qur'an (4:76)[2]

As indicated above, Islam shares its roots with Christianity and Judaism. The religion

was initiated by divine revelations to an Arab man named Mohammed. Mohammed,

while described as a spiritual man by subsequent biographers, was essentially an

animist as were the tribes of Arabia during the dawn of the 7th century AD. During this

experience Mohammed was directed by an angel to recite in the name of God. "When

Mohammed failed to respond, the angel seized him by the throat and shook him as he

repeated the command. Again Mohammed failed to react, so the angel proceeded to

choke him until Mohammed was finally compelled to do as he was told."[3] Not

surprisingly then is this religion named Islam, variously defined as acceptance,

surrender, submission, or commitment.[4] The Muslim, the Islamic adherent, recognizes

the human obligation to achieve God's will on earth.

Mohammed's revelations were ultimately placed together in a single book called the

Qur'an, meaning recitations. Together these recitations lay out the responsibilities of

Muslims, providing a coherent framework for governing one's spiritual life. "The

revelations to Mohammed repeat stories of previous prophets, some of whom are well

known and occur in the Bible and others not so familiar."[5] By sharing Judeo-Christian

---

[2] *The Qur'an: Translation*, trans. M. H. Shakir, (Elmhurst, NY: Tahrike Tarsile Qur'an, Inc., 1991), 55.
[3] *World Religions: From Ancient History to the Present*, rev. ed., ed. Geoffrey Parrinder (New York: Facts on File, 1983), 466.
[4] World Religions, 462.
[5] World Religions, 469.

roots, Islam was meant to be a correction to the wayward path of Christianity, much as Christians view their religion as correcting a flawed implementation of Judaism. In Islam, Jesus is viewed as an important prophet, but not as the embodiment of God on earth. Mohammed is the final and most important prophet in a lengthy prophetic tradition, the seal of the prophets. Therefore, to its adherents, Islam is the final word given to man by God, the Qur'an is the record of that word and its messenger, Mohammed, to be especially revered.

Once complete, the revelations given to Mohammed to recite were conveyed to his fellow citizens of Mecca. In his formal role as prophet, Mohammed initially met with limited success in convincing or converting others. Generally there was no incentive to convert and Mohammed lacked the ability to compel others. To some his recitations, preaching change in relation to their current existence and culture, were bothersome, if not threatening. By preaching a monotheistic doctrine, Mohammed's message had the implication of breaking down tribal divisions which were somewhat sustained by deities unique to each tribe. Additionally Islam carried a message of social justice and fundamental egalitarianism - foreign ideas that obviously had greater appeal to some strata of the society.[6] Ultimately Mohammed and his small band of followers were persecuted in Mecca. As a consequence Mohammed searched for a safer destination to emigrate and selected Yathrib, current day Medina. The migration to Medina is called the *Hejira*. It's importance in Islam is such that it marks the beginning of the Islamic calendar.

Mohammed established the first Muslim community in Medina, called the *Ummah*. Interestingly the Medinese population included some Jewish tribes that were invited into

---

[6] *Islam: Empire of Faith*, produced by Gardner Films in association with PBS and Devillier Donegan Enterprises, Producer/Director Robert Gardner. 180 minutes, 2000, videocassette.

the *Ummah* as well, though they did not convert to Islam. Mohammed met with greater success in converting the Medinese to Islam than he had with the Meccans, and as a result rose to a prominent position in the city. Mohammed felt certain that Jews and Christians would recognize him as their prophet as well. Instead of converting, however, most Jews and Christians viewed Mohammed's teachings as distortions and rejected both his prophecy and his primacy. Mohammed's answer was to eliminate their membership in the *Ummah*, thus causing the first rift between Jews and Muslims.

As his power and authority increased, and as his flock grew, Mohammed began to turn his eyes back towards Mecca. A city whose wealth and strength was built on trade, Mohammed recognized its weakness as its caravans. In ancient Arab tradition and fashion, Mohammed began raiding these caravans. With time, Mecca was weakened such that when Mohammed arrived at the gates, the city capitulated. His first act was to destroy its pagan symbols. This act marked the beginning of the spread of Islam and its rule, and thus, from its earliest days, it was spread by the sword.   This new "...state was led by [Mohammed], the Prophet of God, and guided by divine revelation."[7] In other words, God was the head of state and Mohammed ruled on his behalf.

Islamic roots run deep. Many of the associated traditions date to the timeframe of the original revelations to Mohammed, sometime early in the 7th century AD or earlier. The recent resurgence of Islam, particularly in the last 100 years, carries with it a view that historic traditions should carry more importance in the future. "Far from abandoning their ancient religious heritage, the Muslims have seen its reaffirmation as the key to their future strength and success."[8] This interesting approach to life seems at least slightly counterintuitive to the Westerner who has become accustomed to a secular

---

[7] John L. Esposito, *The Islamic Threat: Myth or Reality,* (New York:Oxford University Press, 1995), 30.
[8] *World Religions*, 506.

world with only nominal reference to religion outside the church. Thus, an important distinction between Islamic and Christian societal and governmental roots is the fundamental interdependence of Islamic traditions with government. On the whole, Islam seems to be the cultural constant and cultural requirement for any Middle Eastern government that seeks legitimacy. [9]

The most telling basis for tradition in Islam is the *Sharia*, or right path of God, essentially Islamic holy law. However, Bernard Lewis also notes that it is a "...magnificent structure of laws, lovingly elaborated by successive generations of jurists and theologians, [and] is one of the major intellectual achievements of Islam."[10] The purpose of *Sharia* is to support the creation of a society in which the faithful can live as God desires and therefore assure themselves of ascension to paradise. *Sharia* is believed to be the manifestation of God's will for man. While the Qur'an, as the divinely revealed and perfect word of God is the single most important document governing man's life, it does not address all aspects of life and has, therefore, been augmented from other sources. If an instance arises which the Qur'an does not adequately address, in consonance with *Sharia*, Muslims next draw from the *Sunnah*, or established practice of Mohammed.[11]

Mohammed is thought to have lived his life as "...a perfect and sinless being."[12] As a consequence, and in the similar tradition of Christians, Muslims following *Sharia* today lead their lives much as Mohammed did--just as Christians aspire to be "Christ-like." Therefore, if the Qur'an fails to reveal a solution to a particular earthly dilemma, then Mohammed's life is used as a guide. Of course the *Sunnah* is codified into a document

---

[9] Fouad Ajami, *The Arab Predicament: Arab Political Thought and Practice Since 1967*, rev. ed. (New York: Cambridge University Press, 1992), 61.

[10] Bernard Lewis, *The Middle East: A Brief History of the Last 2,000 Years* (New York: Touchstone, 1997), 223. Cited hereafter as Lewis, *The Middle East*.

[11] *World Religions*, 482.

[12] *World Religions*, 470.

called the *hadith*, the authoritative documentation of Mohammed's life. Both documents were essentially fixed in the 7th century AD, though the *hadith* was not complete until the 10th century. The circumstance exists, therefore, where situations may develop for which no 7th century equivalent exists.

In this case, Muslims refer to *ijma*, or past consensus. Like common law in the west, Muslims use *ijma*, the representative views of the past community to govern current behavior. The idea is that the "...community will never agree in error."[13] The final mechanism of *Sharia* used by Muslims to govern life is referred to as *Qiyas*, or analogical reasoning. In the event that all else fails, according to the tradition of the *Sharia*, the analog is the best answer. Clearly, a historical example restored analogically will allow for interpretation, and in fairness, "...Muslims managed to a remarkable extent to modify and develop their laws in accordance with the principle laid down by jurists that the rules change as the times change."[14] Thus it is accepted that the past provides the best guide to the future, and that the strength of the current society rests in the wisdom of the past society. This is not an entirely foreign concept to the West, but it does accentuate the historical focus of Islam and gives predictive insight into the constraints governing current Muslim leaders and decision-makers who seek to lead in a manner beyond the confines of the secular and consistent with the expectations of their Muslim followers. But it is also important to recognize that Islam is adaptive and even its strictest adherents will embrace the future so long as they do not deny the past. In other words, it is possible to interject change into the society so long as that change does not challenge or jeopardize any basic Islamic principles.

---

[13] *World Religions*, 492.
[14] Lewis, *The Middle East*, 224.

Though an experience unfamiliar to the West, at least in the past several hundred years, the Muslim tradition is to govern by *Sharia*, or holy law, a condition with which many Muslims are quite comfortable. While Americans take for granted the idea that the government manages secular affairs while the church looks after matters of faith, this has not always been so. "This idea [the separation of church and state] was not entirely new; it had some precedent in the writings of Spinoza, Locke, and the other philosophers of the European Enlightenment. It was in the United States, however, that the principle was first given the force of law and gradually, in the course of two centuries, became a reality."[15] Other methods of social governance exist. In the Muslim view, Islam, and specifically the Qur'an and other culturally derived sources form the basis for governmental decision-making and jurisprudence. While this tradition has been modified somewhat recently to accommodate western business practices, according to Bernard Lewis, "In Muslim teaching and experience, there was no Caesar. God was the head of state, and Mohammed his prophet taught and ruled on his behalf."[16] As will be explored later, history has shown that Muslims tend to vacillate between Islam and more secular forms as the proper foundations for government.

Similarities and differences between the West and the world of Islam do exist. It is interesting, however, that such great culture conflict manifests in an environment where so much commonality likewise exists. Historically, it was the territorial spread of Islam that brought it into conflict with Christendom. However, its territorial spread was accompanied by the conversions of many Christians to Islam, and its tradition as a monotheistic religion made it a competing theology with Christianity. In the one hundred

---

[15] Bernard Lewis, "The Roots of Muslim Rage: Why so many Muslims deeply resent the West, and why their bitterness will not easily be mollified," printed in the Atlantic Monthly, September, 1990, URL: <http://www.theatlantic.com/issues/90sep/rage.htm>. Accessed 3 January 2002. Cited hereafter as Lewis, Muslim Rage.

[16] Lewis, *The Middle East*, 138.

and twenty or so years following the death of Mohammed in 632 AD, the subsequent leaders of Islam, referred to as the rightly guided caliphs, and after them the Umayyad caliphate, extended the Islamic empire to and throughout Spain in the West and to China in the east.

The Roots of Conflict

> *Sovereignty belongs only to God; he is the sole judge and legislator, and anyone who says or thinks otherwise is an infidel.*[17]
>
> -Muhammad Saïd al-Ashmawy

The discussion that emerged from Samuel Huntington's article "The Clash of Civilizations?" questions the inevitability of conflict based on cultural boundaries and differences.[18] It is likely an oversimplification of the complex issues associated with the relationship between Islam and the West, to say that culture is the single facet contributing to conflict between Muslim nations and the West today. However, it is a crucial factor. Among the most important issues fostering clash between these societies is the evolution of the relationship between Christendom and Islam over the last 1,400 or more years. The principal dynamic in this relationship is the expansion of Islam and its formation of a vast and dynamic empire during the first 1,000 years following God's revelation to Mohammed. Muslims are enormously proud of the accomplishments of their forebears, which include the conquest and domination of an empire including all of Northern Africa, the Middle East, South Asia save the tip of the Indian subcontinent, Indonesia and Malaysia, parts of Southeastern Europe and, for a time, Spain and Southern France.[19] Importantly, these conquests weren't simply for the aggrandizement of the Muslim empire, but rather for the purpose of fulfilling God's will on earth, that all people might be brought to the Muslim faith.

Islam as both a religion and system of social governance was originally spread through territorial expansion, much of which was initially, though not exclusively, violent. This

---

[17] Richard Labéviere, *Dollars for Terror: The United States and Islam* (New York: Algora Publishing, 2000), 123.

[18] Samuel Huntington, "The Clash of Civilizations?", *Foreign Affairs Magazine*, Summer, 1993, <http://www.foreignaffairs.org/Search/document.asp?i=19930601FAESSAY5188.XML>, Accessed 1 October, 2001.

[19] See Appendix for Maps of Islam, Expansion of Islamic World 1500 AD.

expansion was nominally ordained by God and was referred to as the *futuh*, meaning openings. Essentially, those outside of Islam, referred to as *dar al-Harb*, the world of war, were opened to *dar al-Islam*, the world of peace and God's promise of salvation. The tenets of Islam envisioned that the entire world would be "opened" to Islam, carrying with it the idea of a beneficent God whose omniscience and omnipotence governed all life on earth. In the Islamic tradition the *futuh* is a commandment of God. Its success was manifest, though not absolute, as it counts among the most enduring empire-building efforts ever witnessed on the globe. Two characteristics of this period are remarkable. One is that it ushered forth a period of enormous scientific and cultural renaissance. The second is that the empire endured, in different forms and under different rulers, for over 1,000 years before its decline. "With the exception of Spain and Sicily, all the territories overrun by Muslims in their first wave of expansion have continued under Muslim dominion until our own time."[20]

According to Pervez Amir Ali Hoodbhoy, "between the 9th and 13th centuries--the Golden Age of Islam--the only people doing decent work in science, philosophy or medicine were Muslims."[21] The contributions of Islamic scholars, scientists and artists are remarkable, and contributed much to later learning and development in the West. While Europe was struggling through the so called Dark Ages, Muslims wrote Arabic dictionaries and poetry; translated and preserved Greek learning that had been all but lost to the West; made substantial advances in medicine, chemistry, astronomy and agronomy; developed, improved or perfected algebra, geometry and trigonometry; and created a rich and vibrant culture that completely outshone Europe at the time.[22]

---

[20] *World Religions*, 476.

[21] Pervez Amir Ali Hoodbhoy, "How Islam Lost its Way: Yesterday's Achievements Were Golden; Today, Reason has been Eclipsed," Washington Post, 30 December 2001, B4.

[22] Lewis, *The Middle East*, 264-267.

Clearly the notion that Arabs or Muslims are or were backwards is an uninformed opinion. "For some eight hundred years Arabic remained the major intellectual and scientific language of the world."[23] During this period Baghdad was the capital of the Abbasid Caliphate, and it became a great center of learning and culture. Under the sponsorship of the caliphs, the works of "...Plato, Aristotle, Hippocrates, Galen, Euclid and Ptolemy..."[24] were translated into Arabic. Astronomers who were 700 years ahead of the West measured the angle of the ecliptic, fixed the position of the stars and determined the length of the solar year.[25] Importantly, "scholars of all races and religions were invited to work [at the Baghdad Academy of Wisdom]. They were concerned with preserving universal heritage, which was not specifically Moslem and was Arabic only in language."[26] At the same time poets and artists also contributed to the works of this period. Among other contributions were erotic odes, love poems and drinking songs, offering some insight into a society somewhat more irreligious and pleasure-oriented than current day trends would suggest.[27] In fact, it may well have been this movement towards more secular pursuits that initiated the revivalist trend. All told, this period had great significance for the Western world as well as Islam, by preserving and passing along ancient learning which otherwise might have been lost. At the same time it figures prominently in the historiography of Islamic culture as a dominant period relative to other cultures, in particular the West.

"The Muslim world in its heyday saw itself as the center of truth and enlightenment, surrounded by infidel barbarians whom it would in due course enlighten and civilize."[28]

---

23 *History of Islam*, <http://www.barkati.net/english/>, accessed 11 January 2002.
24 Gaston Wiet, *Baghdad: Metropolis of the Abbasid Caliphate*,
<http://www.fordham.edu/halsall/med/wiet.html>, accessed 11 January 2002.
25 Wiet, *Baghdad*.
26 Wiet, *Baghdad*.
27 Wiet, *Baghdad*.
28 Lewis, Muslim Rage

Islamic expansion continued in fits and starts from the 7th century until the 17th century. Ultimately its spread threatened Christendom. At the very end of the 11th century, Pope Urban II initiated the first crusade. The threatened collapse of the Byzantine Empire inspired many to sign up for the liberation of Jerusalem. Opportunities for loot and the expiation of sin served as equal motivators for this successful expedition to the Levant. By 1099 the Crusaders had captured Jerusalem, a city they kept as part of the "Latin" empire until 1187 when they were ejected by Salah al-Din. There were crusades which followed the first, totaling eight in all. According to Esposito, "few events had a more shattering and long-lasting effect on Muslim-Christian relations than the Crusades. Five centuries of peaceful coexistence were...shattered by a series of holy wars which pitted Christianity against Islam and left an enduring legacy of distrust and misunderstanding."[29] This relationship dynamic continues today, contributing to the persistence of an unhealthy and unnecessarily difficult relationship between Islam and the West. Islamic radicals today use the term crusader as an emotive tool to describe Westerners and their apparent motivations. "For Muslims, the memory of the Crusades lives on as the clearest example of militant Christianity, an earlier harbinger of the aggression and imperialism of the Christian West, a vivid reminder of Christianity's early hostility toward Islam."[30]

Despite this legacy, the Crusades were a reasonably short-lived incursion into the Islamic world. Beyond the control of Jerusalem, their major concrete effect was, perhaps, to delay the collapse of the Byzantium Empire for several hundred years.[31] Having a more profound temporal and psychological impact on Islamic culture and the

---

[29] Esposito, 39-41. Much of the preceding obtained from Esposito who offers a concise appraisal of this period.

[30] Esposito, 40.

[31] *History of Islam.* Byzantium fell in 1453 to Mehmet the conqueror who captured Constantinople and made it the capital of the Ottoman empire.

subsequent relationship of Islam to the West was European colonialism. "If the first ten centuries [of Islam] seemed a lopsided contest in which Christendom was more often than not literally or figuratively under siege, the dawn of European colonialism signaled a shift in power: thereafter colonialism would dominate the history and psyche of Muslims."[32] "At the height of the European colonial expansion in the 19th century, most of the Islamic world was under colonial rule with the exception of a few regions, such as, the heart of the Ottoman empire, Persia, Afghanistan, Yemen and certain parts of Arabia."[33] The rising strength of the West, particularly in relation to the Islamic world, was a source of fear, resentment and envy for subjugated Muslims. While there was profound regret at the weakness of the Islamic world, there was also a sense that if the secrets of the West could be learned and implemented, they could restore the Islamic world to its former greatness.

In the meantime, European colonialism redrew the map of Islam, and in large measure established the geographic boundaries in effect between nations today.

> In most of the countries of the Middle East the impact of Western domination was indirect but, nevertheless, powerful enough to shatter the old society beyond repair and to initiate a process of violent social, economic, and political change which disrupted the traditional order, destroyed traditional loyalty and relationships, and engendered a deep resentment against the Western standard-bearers of the civilization from which these changes originated.[34]

Lacking historical relevance, these lines between nations have created an environment of questionable legitimacy for some rulers, and have subdivided the early empire in

---

[32] Esposito, 46.

[33] *History of Islam.*

[34] Ajami, 6.

such a fashion that pan-Arab and pan-Islamic movements, while legitimate and historical, must compete with the interests of established nation-states for primacy in the political arena. In other words, the ideal of reestablishing the past greatness of the Islamic empire must overcome the reality of eliminating or marginalizing the established powers before it can be brought into effect. Colonialist roots therefore remain in the post-colonial period.

From the Muslim perspective these roots include the nation of Israel. Today, in some eyes, Israel is seen not just as a relic of the colonial period, but also as a Western-oriented, Western-dependent colony, owing its existence to the partition of Palestine.[35] This cultural perspective, carrying with it enmities and transgressions associated with the Islamic-Western Christendom relationship beginning centuries ago, is emblematic of the mistrust and resentment that continues to dominate relations between Islam and the West today. From this past we get this future. Without overemphasizing the stereotype, it is important to note that many Muslims blame this historical relationship with the West for many of the woes they endure today.

An important juxtaposition in the context of deciphering the impact radical Islam has for U.S. policies is the nature and character of the United States at the dawn of the 21st century. Common wisdom holds that few Americans see recent global or U.S. actions as a conspiracy to destroy Islam. The attack on the World Trade Center and Pentagon on September 11th caught many Americans unawares. Despite the previous attacks on U.S. embassies in Dar es Salaam, Tanzania and Nairobi, Kenya and the attack on the U.S.S. Cole, few Americans were prepared for the lethality of a well-organized, well-financed radical Islamic threat inside the United States.

---

[35] Esposito, 73.

Nonetheless, the rising conflict between cultures that seems to manifest itself at every meeting of a global trade or finance body is aimed at the United States, or, at least, at the forces which seek to maintain the status quo. To the extent that it suits its national interests, America is nothing if not a proponent of the status quo. Loosely defined, this means that America wishes to retain its position of economic dominance in the world. What Americans often do not see is the cultural consequence of globalization. For many foreigners, U.S. policies seek to maintain U.S. dominance at their expense. The significance of this dynamic is the birth of a perception that America is complicit, if not responsible for many of the world's ills. To the extent that the U.S. acts as a hegemon, it reinforces this view. For many, a cogent argument can therefore be formed that the United States is responsible for what ails them.

Among the trends experienced in Muslim nations generally and the Middle East in particular are weak, undiversified economies; imbalanced distribution of wealth; high unemployment; repressive governments offering limited political expression; rapidly growing, increasingly younger populations; and the resurgence of a politicized form of Islam.[36] There are 53 nations or regions (e.g. Gaza and West Bank are included as political divisions in this analysis) that have a majority Muslim population.[37] Of these, only nine countries have per capita Gross Domestic Products (GDPs) above the global average of $7,200: Bahrain, Brunei, Kuwait, Libya, Malaysia, Oman, Qatar, Saudi Arabia and the United Arab Emirates. Of these nine, only one, Malaysia, does not have oil or a petroleum derivative as its primary export. None of the remaining eight nations have even modestly diversified economies. Some of the remaining 53 do have

---

[36] See Appendix A for a listing of these nations or political entities; Appendix B for per capita gross domestic product; Appendix C for their major exports; and Appendix D for unemployment statistics.

[37] *The CIA World Factbook*, 2001, <http://www.cia.gov/cia/publications/factbook/index.html>, accessed 13 January 2002.

diversified economies, but they are poor nations and so the consequences of diversification are relatively meaningless from the perspective of the average citizen.

Coupled with largely underperforming or fragile economies is a growing "youth bulge", an increasingly younger population throughout much of the region. Among the countries in the world with the most significant youth bulge are Afghanistan, Pakistan, Iraq, Gaza, and Yemen. Saudi Arabia, Egypt, Iraq and Oman will have significant youth bulges for the next 20 years.[38] The implications of this demographic trend are potentially severe in light of some of the complicating factors associated with the region. For example, "Algeria's youth bulge contributed to long-lasting civil strife, as youth lacked adequate educational, employment, and housing opportunities. Algeria's unemployment is still more than 30 percent."[39]

The match being held to the powder keg today is the tradition of political repression in many Muslim nations. According to Pervez Amir Ali Hoodbhoy, "Of the 48 countries with a full or near Muslim majority, none has yet evolved a stable democratic political system...all Muslim countries are dominated by...corrupt elites who...advance their personal interests. None of these countries has a viable educational system or a university of international stature."[40] Interestingly, despite an admonition from the Qur'an for the ruler to consult with his citizens, the trend today is authoritarian rule. In fairness, this situation is not new. Bemoaning the transition from the Umayyad caliphate to the Abassid caliphate in 750 AD, one Ibn Qutayba is thought to have said: "Our leadership which was consultative, has become arbitrary. Our succession, which

---

[38] *Longterm Global Demographic Trends: Reshaping the Geopolitical Landscape*, 1991, <http://www.cia.gov/cia/publications/Demo_Trends_For_Web.pdf>, Accessed 6 January 2002.
[39] *Longterm Global Demographic Trends.*
[40] Hoodbhoy, "How Islam Lost its Way," B4.

was by choice of the community, is now by inheritance."[41] Today this situation appears much the same. Fouad Ajami complained that "...everywhere in that large Arab world, the political discourse is a monologue."[42]

The issue, though, isn't necessarily a comparative one--either to view Muslim governments through the eyes of liberal Western democracy, or through the urgings of the *Qur'an* or the *hadith*. The implications for the stated demographic trends and purported governmental repression are really for the Muslim citizen to decide. Interestingly, Muslims, in particular Middle Eastern Muslims, have chosen various options for governments, alternating between Western models of socialism or nationalism with more traditional Islamic governments partly- or wholly-based on the *Sharia*. Efforts at establishing a purely secular, nationalistic ideological foundation in the Middle East have met with only limited success. For example, both Syria and Iraq are the product of the Ba'athist movement that sought to implant a secular, western style government in Arab countries. In both cases, the party and the country were co-opted by their respective militaries, subordinating national needs to military needs, and politicizing the military to the point of military uselessness. Other secular, Western-oriented examples abound, such as Algeria, Egypt, Lebanon, Libya, Malaysia, and Pakistan to name a few. The interesting trend, though, is that few Muslim nations, and perhaps only Turkey today, endeavor to be completely secular. The trend, even in secular regimes, is to appeal to Islam for legitimacy. In documenting this trend, Fouad Ajami said: "...the more popular nationalism became, the more it identified with Islam."[43]

---

[41] Lewis, *The Middle East*, 144.
[42] Ajami, 27
[43] Ajami, 61.

However, every nation in the Islamic world today has a movement based on political Islam, the goal being to replace the current, supposedly illegitimate, government with one consistent with the *Sharia*, Islamic holy law. Examples of successful movements are Iran under the Ayatollah Khomeini and, until recently, Afghanistan under the Taliban. Clearly the roots of political Islam exist within the tradition of Islam. It also seems apparent that political repression in Muslim nations can engender a radicalized movement towards political Islam, essentially an effort to achieve political expression in the only manner possible. Radical Muslims have identified Islam as the target of a coordinated and determined Western attack. While this idea is not necessarily universally accepted as reality--or even completely defensible--it serves well as an emotive political tool to create a supportive worldview. However, it is a fatalistic world view demanding a call to action. "Modern thinkers believe Islam, when truly understood, to be an imperative to determined action."[44] The idea of Islam under attack is unquestionably a view held by many Muslims. However, as with anything, there are two sides to the issue. Most Westerners look with some surprise upon the claim that Islam has suffered intentional and systematic attacks with an aim towards destroying not only a culture and way of life, but the true expression of God to man. Many Muslims hold that there were three crusades, the most recent one still ongoing. Fouad Ajami characterizes these as the original Christian crusades that aimed to retrieve the Christian holy lands; the Western colonialism, beginning with Napoleon's invasion of Egypt in 1798; and the modernism (though not so termed by Ajami) that is manifested by globalization, increased international economic interdependence, and a broad-based introduction of foreign culture, values and belief systems into Muslim countries.[45] In the search for a solution to end Western dominance, Muslims have increasingly begun to look into the past, towards the Golden Age of Islam.

---

[44] *World Religions*, 506.
[45] Ajami, 62.

Islamic Revivalism

> *For, as Muslim theology maintains, Allah will help and sympathize only when the*
> *believers do their part.* [46]
>
> ⁻Fouad Ajami

The idea of revivalism is not new in Islam, in fact, it is a recurring trend. Islamic society seems to evince a path towards fundamentalist interpretations of Islam and then away from Islam and towards Western secular models. The constant in this pattern is an intent to successfully compete against Western cultural, political and economic dominance. From the time of Mohammed Al-Ghazali in the late 11th century to the present, the sine wave of Islamic revivalism has manifested itself with increasing frequency. For U.S. policy makers, the nature of this trend is important for its predictability and resilience. To the Western mind, the importance of Islam to legitimize government in Muslim nations and to act as a bona fide alternative to other governmental types is, at best, confusing, if not a non sequitur. This paradigm will have to be overcome to develop effective and successful U.S. foreign policy. Over time, Islam has served as a yardstick by which governmental legitimacy could be gauged by Muslims. The increasingly secular nature of the Abassid caliphate motivated this first movement.

Mohammed al-Ghazali, the "reviver of the faith", lived from 1059 until 1111 AD.[47] He became a renowned Islamic scholar, later drifting into mysticism. He initiated a revivalist movement that, according to some, brought to a close the period of scientific and cultural innovation and scholarship referred to as the Islamic Golden Age. According to Hoodbhoy, "...in the 12th century, Muslim orthodoxy reawakened, spearheaded by the Arab cleric Imam al-Ghazali. Al-Ghazali championed revelation

---

[46] Ajami, 8.
[47] Lewis, *The Middle East,* 240.

over reason, predestination over free will. He damned mathematics as being against Islam, an intoxicant of the mind that weakened the faith." [48] Al-Ghazali's fundamental view of Islam was based on a literal interpretation of the *Qur'an*, "...he believed the [Qur'an] said exactly what it meant, and sought only to provide the arguments that would convince others of the truth of the revelation."[49] The lesson that emerges for later generations, though, is that Islam achieved the apex of its civilization at the point of its most conspicuous and faithful observance of the strictures of Islam. The connection with God, faithfulness and earthly success are inextricably linked in the worldview of political Islam. It follows, therefore, that a return to faithfulness will achieve a corresponding return to a position of cultural, economic, scientific, political and military dominance.

Al-Ghazali's revivalist movement coincided with the first Christian Crusade around 1099. It may be academically disingenuous to suggest that Al-Ghazali's motivation was as a response to the crusade. All indications are that Al-Ghazali was simply motivated by the differences between his conflicting perceptions of reality and the practice of religion during his time. However, the revivalist movements that followed Al-Ghazali's are directly linked to a Western cause in Islam. Beginning before the period of Western colonialism, there was a recurring search for governmental methods that would yield success against Western hegemony. The failure of Western models to succeed in this regard was repeatedly followed by movements espousing political Islam. Among these were the Mahdi of Sudan (1848-1885); the Sanusi of Libya (1787-1859); the Wahhabi of Saudi Arabia (1703-1792); the Fulani of Nigeria (1754-1817); the Faraidiyyah of Hajji

---

[48] Hoodbhoy, "How Islam Lost its Way," B4.
[49] *World Religions*, 488.

Shariat Allah of Bengal (1764-1840); the Ahmad Brelwi of India (1786-1831); and the Padri of Indonesia (1803-1837).[50]

The basis for political Islam then, was that the "...existing political, economic and social systems had failed."[51] As a result, the philosophical and ideological foundation of these movements became: "...(1) Islam was the solution; (2) a return to the Qur'an and the *Sunnah* of the Prophet was the method; (3) a community governed by God's revealed law, the *Sharia*, was the goal; and (4) all who resisted, Muslim or non-Muslim, were enemies of God."[52] Despite the relative decline against the West, these early revivalists viewed the cause of this decline as internal to the community. According to Esposito, "The cause was identified as Muslim departure from true Islamic values brought about by the infiltration and assimilation of local, indigenous, un-Islamic beliefs and practices."[53]

Following the 18th and 19th century revivalists, a third movement arose during the early 20th century. The initiation of this period began from a perception of the failure of the Western, liberal, nationalist government models that did not bring about a return to the great society or achieve success consistent with expectations. The two prominent movements during this period were the Muslim Brotherhood of Egypt, formed in 1928 and still a viable political movement today; and the Jamaat-i-Islami (Islamic Society) of South Asia.[54] Both movements were highly critical of the West and the application of Western political movements or systems of governance to the Islamic world. According

---

[50] Esposito, 50.
[51] Esposito, 14.
[52] Esposito, 50.
[53] Esposito, 50.
[54] Esposito, 69.

to Esposito, "Both the Brotherhood and the Jamaat emphasized Islam's ideological self-sufficiency...", and sought to replace current governments with Islamic ones.[55]

The fourth revivalist trend followed the 1967 Arab-Israeli war in which the Israelis won an overwhelming victory against the Arabs. Of the nations arrayed against Israel, Egypt, Syria and Iraq were all led by nationalist movements. Egypt under Nasser was the leader in the Arab world and was the national advocate for Nasser's pan-Arab political philosophy. Both Iraq and Syria were Ba'athist, a governmental system of political nationalism. Until the war was lost, "the struggle against Israel symbolized the battle against imperialism, provided a common cause and sense of unity, and distracted from the failures of regimes and of Arab nationalism/socialism."[56] After the war, the humiliation of such a crushing defeat caused a period of soulful introspection, the result of which, almost universally was, once again, a rejection of Western influence and Western systems of governance. The defeat was "...an indictment of Arab nationalism, [it] further inflamed Arab and Muslim passions against Israel and American neoimperialism, and became a major catalyst for the Islamic resurgence."[57]

The idea of Islamic revivalism is simply motive force for change. Much of the energy for revivalist Islam is the same as it has been for hundreds of years:

> ...a sense that existing political, economic, and social systems had failed; a
> disenchantment with, and at times a rejection of, the West; a quest for identity
> and greater authenticity; and the conviction that Islam provides a self-sufficient
> ideology for state and society, a valid alternative to secular nationalism, socialism
> and capitalism.[58]

---

[55] Esposito, 69.
[56] Esposito, 73.
[57] Esposito, 75.
[58] Esposito, 14.

Among other things, it is their history as a great society that has caused Muslims to look rearward and outward for correcting solutions, answers to their current problems vis à vis the West. The point of all of this is not only the question of survival, which to most Muslims likely seems moot, but rather the restoration of greatness, recognized as the need to successfully compete against the various threats which have manifested against Islam, beginning about three hundred years ago.

The forces for change can become radicalized. Islam, in its most basic sense refers to an obligation to submit. In its religious sense, it demands "...an attitude of humble recognition of the human obligation to fulfill the purpose of the majestic and all-powerful Creator."[59] The principal notion here is that the person able to define God's will, particularly as it relates to events since the 7th century, all of which are subject to a post-Qur'anic interpretation, is also able to invoke a sense of obligation to duty. Coupled with traditions such as *jihad*, this combination is a powerful and effusive force, particularly for a Muslim without a well-established worldview--or for a Muslim who has a strong cultural tradition and a weak rational tradition. Much is made of the *jihad* in the west. Literally, a struggle, *jihad* is widely translated as holy war. Traditionally "The Muslim *jihad*...was perceived as unlimited, as a religious obligation that would continue until all the world had either adopted the Muslim faith or submitted to Muslim rule."[60] Of course the fear in the West today is not so much based on the idea of being offered the choice of enslavement or conversion, or of being subjugated by proselytizing Muslims, but rather the inscrutability and apparent unpredictability of a people motivated to kill themselves and others for an idea which lacks a clear Western translation.

---

[59] *World Religions*, 462.
[60] Lewis, *The Middle East*, 233.

Based on recent events, it is apparent that a fifth revivalist movement is occurring today. While it may simply be a continuation of the post-1967 period, some unique factors contribute to the idea that the movement is distinct. Among these are the rapid rise of the United States to economic, military and cultural dominance, if not hegemony, in the post-cold war period; the significant number of conflicts in the past 10 years involving Muslim nations ; and a marked increase in radical Islamic organization and effectiveness. According to Osama bin Laden, Muslim conflicts include "...Tajikistan, Burma, Cashmere, Assam, Philippine, Fatani, Ogadin, Somalia, Eritrea, Chechnya and Bosnia-Herzegovina."[61] Whatever the various causes, there are clear forces for change, many of which, such as *al-Qaeda* and its member organizations, are radicalized.[62] Despite the obvious tendencies towards radicalization, it is important to note that the great traditions in Islam stand against this trend. Radicalization of Islamic revivalism is not a necessary dynamic and is probably avoidable. It certainly need not take on the level of influence it has at present.

---

[61] Yonah Alexander and Michael S. Swetnam, *Usama bin Laden's al-Qaida: Profile of a Terrorist Network* (Ardsley, NY: Transnational Publishers, Inc., 2001), 65.

[62] From Webster's Revised Unabridged Dictionary (1913): One who advocates radical changes in government or social institutions, especially such changes as are intended to level class inequalities; -- opposed to conservative.

Radical Islam

> *The ruling to kill the Americans and their allies--civilian and military--is an*
> *individual duty for every Muslim who can do it in any country in which it is*
> *possible to do it...*[63]
>
> -Osama bin Laden

Chiefly in response to Western colonialism, and specifically the British presence in Egypt, Hassan al-Banna, a twenty-two year old teacher from Ismailia, founded the Muslim Brotherhood in 1928.[64] The Brotherhood was established to encourage the development of an Islamic government in Egypt. The movement was rapidly internationalized and spread to Sudan, Palestine, Jordan, Lebanon, Syria, Algeria and many of the Gulf states by the 1940s. The goals of the movement included economic and social reform, all of which was premised upon observance of the rules of Islam. Importantly, the Muslim Brotherhood sought to use Islam as "...a means of overcoming social and economic injustice imposed by the 'secular' controllers of the state."[65] The Muslim Brotherhood ushered in the modern era of political Islam, or as it is often referred to, Islamism. It became the most important movement of its kind and rapidly subsumed similar, nascent movements in Egypt and elsewhere. It remains a potent political force throughout the Muslim world today.

Among the changes to the ancient Muslim world caused by colonization and Westernization was the elimination of the Ottoman caliphate by Gemal Attaturk in 1924. Attaturk's view was entirely secular, and as he sought to establish a globally competitive nation-state, a modern Turkey, he viewed Islam as an impediment to success. By

---

[63] Alexander and Swetnam, B2.

[64] Labévière, 127. Much of the description of the Muslim Brotherhood comes from Labévière.

[65] Sarah Ansari, "The Islamic World in the Era of Western Domination," in *The Cambridge Illustrated History of the Islamic World*, ed. Francis Robinson (Cambridge, England: Cambridge University Press, 1996), 112.

eliminating the caliphate, Attaturk disposed of a potent force in Islam, a rallying post for Muslim unity, but concurrently he freed himself and his nation from the strict constraints associated with Islamic theocracy. Only four or five years later, Hassan al-Banna saw the "...reestablishment of the caliphate as the only framework that could be effective in uniting all the believers..."[66] As the father of the modern Islamist movement, al-Banna established political objectives which remain active and relevant today. Al-Banna's Islamism forms the ideological basis for political Islam today, including radical Islamic movements of which there are literally dozens throughout the world. Perhaps the best known of such movements today is Osama bin Laden's *al-Qaeda*.

Al-Qaeda was established by bin Laden during the war between the Afghani *Mujahideen* and the Soviet Union as a support network for the Arab volunteers fighting in that conflict.[67] In some ways it is but an exemplar of the sorts of movements and ideologies that emerged from the Afghan *jihad*. As many as 50,000 volunteers from throughout the Muslim world were recruited to participate in the war, chiefly by appealing to their sense of duty in the defense of fellow Muslims.[68] These Muslims, later called "Afghan-Arabs", became the tools of U.S., Saudi and Pakistani foreign policy, insofar as they were fighting a proxy war against the Soviet Union. Many of these *Mujahideen* were introduced to a fiery ideology at *madrassas*, or theological schools, set up in Pakistani border towns. They were then trained at camps in Pakistan and, later in the war, in Afghanistan. The curriculum, inspired by the U.S. Central Intelligence Agency, included weapons handling, bomb-making and similar skills.[69] From the war, Afghan-Arabs have returned to their countries of origin and either begun,

---

[66] Labévière, 126.

[67] Alexander and Swetnam, 4.

[68] John K. Cooley, *Unholy Wars: Afghanistan, America and International Terrorism,* 2nd ed. (Sterling, VA: Pluto Press, 2000), 4.

[69] Cooley, 90-91.

joined or influenced radical Islamic insurgencies with the aim of overthrowing their current governments and replacing them with Islamic governments which uphold *Sharia*.

Not without some reason, these Afghan-Arabs were confident that they could achieve their daunting aims. Consistent with their ideology, with God on their side they had defeated a superpower, which not only left the battlefield, but shortly thereafter, collapsed as a nation. They felt that as long as God was with them, no one could stand against them. Shortly after the Afghan war, Algerian veterans returned home and joined together to overthrow the Algerian government. In 1991 the Islamic Salvation Front captured 60% of the parliamentary seats in an open election.[70] In January of 1992 the Army canceled the election results and declared presidential rule. The civil war that ensued claimed 100,000 lives by the end of last decade.[71] The Arab-Afghans later organized themselves into the Armed Islamic Group and took the lead in the civil war.

In Egypt, in November of 1997, Afghan-Arabs massacred 58 foreign tourists at the ancient Egyptian city of Luxor as part of an overall effort to weaken Egypt by destroying its tourist trade. Afghan-Arabs fought in Bosnia, Kosovo and Chechnya. Today ethnic Chinese Uighurs, who gained experience in Afghanistan, fight for an independent Eastern Turkestan in the Chinese province of Xinjiang.[72] Likewise, according to Rashid, Filipino Moros, Uzbeks, Saudis, Kuwaitis and others came "...to fight the *jihad* with the *Mujahideen* and to train in weapons, bomb-making and military tactics so they could take the *jihad* back home.[73]

---

[70] Ahmed Rashid, *Taliban: Militant Islam, Oil & Fundamentalism in Central Asia* (New Haven, CT: Yale University Press, 2001), 135.
[71] Cooley, 6.
[72] Cooley, 4.
[73] Rashid, 128.

Today *al-Qaeda* appears to have assumed a position of leadership in the radical Islamic movement, coordinating and funding the efforts of like-minded groups in the Muslim world, and apparently carrying out attacks against Western interests, specifically the United States. In May of 1996 bin Laden "...declared a holy war on the government of the United States because it is unjust, criminal and tyrannical."[74] In a *fatwa*, or religious edict issued by bin Laden and the senior leadership of *al-Qaeda*, he identified his complaints against the United States: the occupation and plunder of the Arabian Peninsula; U.S. attempts to "massacre" the Iraqi people; and U.S. support for Israel and its "...occupation of Jerusalem."[75]

On the surface, though, *al-Qaeda's* political objectives differ little from al-Banna's Muslim Brotherhood circa 1928. According to the *Chandigarh Tribune*, bin Laden has said that it is "a sacred objective of *Al-Qaida*...to unite all Muslims and establish a government which follows the rule of the Caliphs."[76] Consistent with this objective, *al-Qaeda*, has established relationships with radical Islamic insurgents throughout the world. According to the United States Department of State, *al-Qaeda* works "...with allied Islamic extremist groups to overthrow regimes it deems 'non-Islamic' and expel Westerners and non-Muslims from Muslim countries."[77] *Al-Qaeda* is thought to be responsible for the World Trade Center bombing in February, 1993; attacks on U.S. troops in Somalia in October, 1993; the Khobar Tower bombings in Saudi Arabia in June, 1996; the bombing of the U.S. Embassies in Kenya and Tanzania in August of

---

[74] Labévière, 107.

[75] Alexander and Swetnam, B1-B3.

[76] "Laden Has Network in 55 Nations," *Chandigarh Tribune* (Chandigarh, India) , 8 June, 2001, URL: <http://www.tribuneindia.com/2001/20010608/world.htm#4>, accessed 4 February 2002.

[77] United States Department of State, *Patterns of Global Terrorism 2000* (Washington D.C.:Department of State Publication 10822, 2001), 68. Cited hereafter as Department of State, *Patterns.*

1998; the bombing of the U.S.S. Cole in October 2000; and the airliner attacks on the World Trade Towers and Pentagon in September, 2001.

It is fair to wonder how these actions promote the goal of a pan-Islamic caliphate, and why the caliphate might be useful today. The caliphate began upon the death of the prophet Mohammed, and was a response to the need for leadership of the *Ummah*. Like Mohammed, the caliphs originally were both the political and theological leaders of the community of believers, but this role evolved over time. Despite the fact that the caliph al-Mamun, 25th of his kind, felt that "...the caliphal state would not survive without [his] unquestioned supreme authority over all matters, religious as well as worldly," the caliphs ultimately gave over religious authority and interpretation to the *ulama*, the loose collection of Islamic scholars.[78] The authority of the caliphs, therefore, was basically secular. According to Bernard Lewis, the task of the caliph was to "...uphold and protect [the faith]--to create conditions in which his subjects could follow the good Muslim life..." and assure themselves of entrance to paradise.[79] Certainly the caliph upheld *Sharia*, religious law, but he did not interpret the sources of that law, the *ulama* did.

In comparison to the many methods Muslim nations have used to govern themselves over the past 100 years, the caliphate represents a uniquely Islamic government. It is therefore a legitimate form of political power and organization for the Muslim who seeks cultural authenticity. It is reminiscent of the glory of ancient Islam, and therefore serves as a compelling model for a future Islamic state. It came from and thrived during a pan-Islamic period, one which had little to no regard for ethnicities, races or the national boundaries that divide Muslims today. However, it remains to be seen whether the

---

[78] Basim Musallam, "The Ordering of Muslim Societies," in *The Cambridge Illustrated History of the Islamic World*, ed. Francis Robinson (Cambridge, England: Cambridge University Press, 1996), 176-178.
[79] Lewis, *The Middle East*, 138.

philosophy of pan-Islamism is truly ecumenical, and how the dissolution of political boundaries would succeed at being "everyone's Islam," that is, account for the Sunni-Shi'a split, among others.

The most vivid example of a future controlled by bin Laden, and a country that offers some insight into both the political ends and means of *al-Qaeda*, is the Taliban's Afghanistan. The overarching vision of the Taliban was to create a place where the choices associated with a secular lifestyle were eliminated and everyone was compelled by the state to submit to a single, strict interpretation of God's will. In the Taliban's view the purpose for the state was to ensure Muslims entrance into paradise, not to perform the range of tasks one typically associates with a modern nation-state. In that sense, the Taliban was not a political party, rather "...cleansers and purifiers...of an Islamic way of life that had been compromised by corruption and excess."[80]

Many of the Taliban were born during the Soviet war in Afghanistan in refugee camps located just over the Pakistani border with Afghanistan.[81] In an environment of dire poverty and no real opportunities for assimilation into Pakistani society or return to Afghanistan, some of them were educated in the hundreds of *madrassas* or Islamic theology schools. In many cases the schools were funded by the Saudi Arabian government, whose policies promoting the export of their interpretation of Islam, *wahabbism*, meshed conveniently with the refugees need for education. *Talib* means student. Taliban is the plural, or students. According to Ahmed Rashid, "...from their *madrassas* they learnt about the ideal Islamic society created by the prophet Mohammed 1,400 years ago."[82] It is important to note that *wahabbism* is a very strict

---

[80] Rashid, 23.

[81] Much of what follows is based on Rashid, 23-29.

[82] Rashid, 23.

and intolerant form of Islam. The extremely repressive society that the Taliban created was in many ways a grotesque caricature of Islam, yet an example that other radical Islamic movements today seek to emulate. "For Muslims everywhere Saudi support for the Taliban [was] deeply embarrassing, because the Taliban's interpretation of Islam [was] so negative and destructive."[83]

Some of the elements of this society include, as mentioned, a real lack of state structures and organizations, the sorts of things most Westerners would take for granted. The Taliban's view was that God would provide what was necessary. They destroyed or banned all forms of entertainment, and compelled men to grow beards and maintain other outward signs of piety. However, the repression of women was much more severe and inconsistent with the treatment they received in any other Muslim nation in the world. According to the Physicians for Human Rights:

> After taking control of the capital city of Kabul on September 26, 1996, the
> Taliban issued edicts forbidding women to work outside the home, attend school,
> or to leave their homes unless accompanied by a husband, father, brother, or
> son. In public, women must be covered from head to toe in a *burqa*, a body-
> length covering with only a mesh opening to see and breathe through. Women
> are not permitted to wear white (the color of the Taliban flag) socks or white
> shoes, or shoes that make noise while women are walking. Also, houses and
> buildings in public view must have their windows painted over if females are
> present in these places.[84]

---

[83] Rashid, 211.

[84] The Physicians for Human Rights, *1999 Report: The Taliban's War on Women - A Health and Human Rights Crisis in Afghanistan*, URL: <http://www.phrusa.org/research/health_effects/exec.html>, accessed 6 February 2002.

As introverted as they were, the Taliban posed a real danger to the outside world. Their provision of safe haven to radical Muslims from throughout the world gave rise to a number of virulently anti-Western organizations and a period of unprecedented cooperation with them--a period in which we still live. *Al-Qaeda* has bridged the gap among many organizations, having linkages to *Al Gamaa-I-Islamiyya* in Egypt, the National Islamic Front in Sudan, *Hezbollah* in Lebanon, *Hamas* in Palestine, *Harakat-ul-Mujahidin* of Pakistan, the Islamic Movement of Uzbekistan, as well as groups from Chechnya, Bangladesh, the Philippines, Algeria, Kenya, Pakistan and on and on. And, importantly, Muslim insurgents have a real following in many countries. In Mao's parlance, the radical Muslim insurgent is the fish swimming in the ocean of the people, and the people are willing.[85] According to the U.S. Department of State, for example, Hamas has tens of thousands of supporters and sympathizers.[86]

It is difficult to overestimate the role that Afghanistan has played in what has become a transnational Islamic insurgency. Initially as a catalyst and later as a sustainer of this movement, Afghanistan likewise is a unifying experience for tens of thousands of Muslims who have trained and fought there with their brothers from around the world. To these people, Afghanistan is where a superpower was defeated. Afghanistan is where the first state of bin Laden's pan-Islamic caliphate was born. Initially the recipient of billions of dollars of Saudi and U.S. aid, Afghanistan has become the wellspring of global terrorism, much of which is focused against Saudi Arabia and the U.S. "The Saudi export of Wahabbism has now boomeranged back home and is increasingly undermining the authority of the royal family.[87] Importantly, bin Laden's goals extend beyond just Saudi Arabia. According to Rashid, he "...[trained]...a second generation of

---

[85] Mao Tse-tung, "Yu Chi Chan (Guerilla Warfare)" in *Mao Tse Tung on Guerilla Warfare (FMFRP 12-18)*, trans. Brigadier General Samuel B. Griffith, (Quantico, VA: United States Marine Corps, 1989), 93.
[86] Department of State, *Patterns*, 60.
[87] Rashid, 211.

Arab-Afghans to bring about an Islamic revolution in Arab countries."[88] It is difficult to know for certain how sustainable the global insurgency is now that the Taliban have been defeated in Afghanistan. However, *al-Qaeda* has bases around the world and appears to be sufficiently well financed and resolute to fight for some time.[89]

We do know that Abu Sayyaf in the Philippines remains active, attacking targets during the 2001 visit of U.S. servicemen to that country to discuss ways to defeat the insurgency. Another associated organization, Hamas, is a virulent threat to Israel, has participated extensively in the Palestinian *intifatah*, or uprising, which began during September 2000, and maintains in their charter the objective foiling the Israeli-Palestinian peace process.[90] *Al-Qaeda* is reputed to have established sleeper cells throughout the world, waiting for an opportunity to strike American and other Western targets. *Al-Qaeda's* timeline is much longer than the four years upon which the average American President must focus as a planning horizon. As a consequence, the terrorist can be much more patient and much more calculating. He can continue to strike and harass; to recruit, ideologize and radicalize his following; and to work towards the acquisition of weapons of mass effect. According to Reuters, bin Laden has sought nuclear weapons for a decade.[91] The challenge for the United States is to stay engaged in the Muslim world, and to develop policies that will reduce or eliminate the threat posed by radical Islam by working to remove its sources.

---

[88] Rashid, 134.

[89] Thomas E. Ricks, "U.S. Eyes Military Assistance for Yemen: Counterterrorism Aid to Philippines Cited as Model," *The Washington Post*, 28 February 2002, A1+.

[90] Christopher C. Harmon, *Terrorism Today* (Portland, Oregon: Frank Cass Publishers, 2000), 30.

[91] "Report: Bin Laden May Have Been Duped by Swindlers," Reuters, 26 February 2002. URL: <http://story.news.yahoo.com/news?tmpl=story&u=/nm/20020226/ts_nm/attack_nuclear_report_dc_1>. Accessed 2 March 2002.

Policy Formulation

> *Where equality exists, there no principality can be established; nor can a republic be established where there is no equality.*
>
> -Niccolo Machiavelli[92]

This review of historical Islam and its political manifestation today, especially in its radical form, should offer some insight into the challenge associated with developing effective U.S. foreign policy in the region. The latest version of the United States' National Security Strategy, dated 2000, offers three core national security objectives: to enhance America's security at home and abroad; to promote America's economic prosperity; and to promote democracy and human rights abroad.[93] Simply as a matter of its own interest, the U.S. is compelled to evaluate the ways in which it can reduce that threat. Similarly, and consistent with its second goal, the U.S. stands to benefit economically by fostering greater economic development outside of its borders, creating both suppliers and consumers for its own products. These first two goals are integrated effectively under the umbrella of the third: democratic transition. They are all complementary in the Muslim world, particularly the Middle East, and all of them center on the issues of political and social stability. While some may argue that U.S. intervention in the affairs of sovereign nations is, at best, inappropriate, it is apparent that the social and political conditions that exist in some nations present a direct threat to the security of the United States. According to President Franklin Delano Roosevelt, "...we have learned that we cannot live alone at peace. We have learned that our own

---

[92] Niccolo Machiavelli, *History of Florence and of the Affairs of Italy: From the Earliest Times to the Death of Lorenzo the Magnificent*, ed. John Bickers, accessed online at URL: <ftp://ibiblio.org/pub/docs/books/gutenberg/etext01/hflit10.txt>. Accessed on 23 Feb 2002.

[93] The White House, *A National Security Strategy for a Global Age*, (Washington, DC:GPO, 2000), 1. Cited hereafter as White House, *Global Age*.

well-being is dependent on the well being of other nations far away. We have learned to be citizens of the world, members of the human community."[94]

The question that follows this assertion is how the United States may be able to accomplish it goals? The theory is fairly straightforward. For example, foreign economic investment and interaction follows stable domestic political environments. Full participation in the global economy should contribute to every participant's betterment, or so economic theory would indicate: maximum economic benefit is derived from the most "...efficient use or management of limited productive resources to achieve maximum satisfaction of human material wants."[95] As a consequence, every nation stands to benefit by focusing their productive potential towards their most efficiently produced products. Truly democratic nations that foster an environment of equality benefit by being able to exploit the highest potential of each of their citizens. In the real world domestic politics represented by public policy and political constituencies has a dampening effect on the potential of any nation to attain its maximum economic benefit. Even in this context it has been shown that the nations of the Muslim world, and of the Middle East in particular, have failed to achieve their economic potential.

Likewise, the security of the United States would be more certainly satisfied by friendly *and* stable political situations abroad. It is an accepted fact that democratic government can contribute to stability and wealth--perhaps more than any other factor. According to the United States Department of State, "...democracy helps create a more secure, stable, and prosperous global arena in which the United Sates can advance its

---

[94] The White House, *A National Security Strategy for a New Century* (Washington D.C.:The White House, 1999), iii. Cited hereafter as White House, *New Century.* Available online as a portable document file at <http://www.dtic.mil/doctrine/jel/other_pubs/nssr99.pdf>. Alternatively available at <http://usinfo.state.gov/regional/ar/natsec2k.htm>. Both accessed on 23 Feb, 2002.

[95] Campbell R. McConnell and Stanley L. Brue, *Economics: Principles, Problems and Policies* (New York: McGraw Hill, inc., 1996), 1.

interests..." and "...is the one national interest that helps secure all the others."[96]   This view inextricably links American interests with American values. So, in the end, fostering democracy in the region should contribute measurably to the accomplishment of the two preceding goals: the enhancement of American security and the sustainment of American prosperity.

While the exportation of democracy and other values and institutions Americans espouse has its adherents around the world, there are many impediments to the establishment of democracy in the Middle East. According to Robin Wright, who comments frequently on the subject of democratization in this region, "...the largest single regional bloc holding out against the global trend toward political pluralism comprises the Muslim countries of the Middle East and North Africa."[97] Interestingly. most countries in the Muslim world claim status as democracies, typically as republics. However, few meet the accepted definition completely: "A state in which the sovereign power resides in the whole body of the people, and is exercised by representatives elected by them..."[98]

The principal challenges to democratic establishment and maturation in the Muslim world, particularly among the nations of the Middle East are entrenched interests and limited experience. Entrenched interests simply refer to the reluctance of governments already in power to hand over control. Again, according to Robin Wright, "...most Muslim societies have no local history of democracy on which to draw. As democracy has blossomed in Western states over the past three centuries, Muslim societies have

---

[96] U.S. Department of State Bureau of Democracy, Human Rights and Labor, *Democracy*, URL: <http://www.state.gov/g/drl/democ/>. Accessed 22 February 2002.

[97] Robin Wright, "Islam and Liberal Democracy: Two Visions of Reformation," *Journal of Democracy*, Spring 1996, 64.

[98] From Webster's Revised Unabridged Dictionary, 1913, under the term "republic."

usually lived under colonial rulers, kings, or tribal and clan leaders."[99] As a consequence, in many cases Muslims simply lack the tools that appropriate political education can provide. In other cases, the seeds of democracy have been sown, but they are carefully harvested by today's rulers to avoid an over abundant crop.

Many unfortunate consequences flow from the very real and very effective manner in which undemocratic governments limit political evolution and liberalization in their countries. Authoritarian governments, in the Middle East in particular, limit the development of robust civil society by controlling non-governmental organizations and political parties. In some cases they limit effective political opposition by requiring all political parties and non-governmental associations to be registered with the government. Failure to register an organization or party is therefore illegal and can be punished. Accordingly, any independent political expression is effectively eliminated or repressed.

Likewise, they limit the audience for the expression of dissenting viewpoints by controlling the media. Al Jazeera headquartered in Qatar offers a wholly new experience for the average Arab who can now gain access to a new world of ideas simply by mounting a satellite dish.[100] Heretofore most people in the region were exposed only to those views officially approved by the government. In a democratic society, "the importance of the media as an avenue for the dissemination of information as well as a vehicle for communicating ideas, educating, polling, debating and discussing cannot be underestimated. A crippled media is a crippled means of information and debate."[101]

---

[99] Wright, 65.

[100] This is an illegal act in some countries in the region, including Iraq.

[101] International Institute for Democracy and Electoral Advice (International IDEA), *Democracy in the Arab world: Challenges, Achievements and Prospects.* (Stockholm: International IDEA, 2000), 7. URL:

Authoritarian regimes in the region enact laws but control their implementation through a weak judiciary. They hold "carefully monitored" elections, and "control" the results. "A common excuse promulgated by non-democratic leaders is that the Arab people do not know what is good for them and they might therefore abuse democracy, were it not controlled."[102] They profoundly limit the participation of women in government. "...The fact that half of the population does not enjoy equal access to decision-making occupations constitutes a serious and, indeed, unacceptable bar to any democratic endeavor."[103]

Many governments in the region use religion, specifically Islam, to support their governments. "In Saudi Arabia, Islam's tenets have been selectively shaped to sustain an authoritarian monarchy."[104] The Saudi's very close ties to the strict *Wahabbi* sect of Islam as a source of political legitimacy have also created an environment of religious intolerance in their country. Among other impediments, religious intolerance offers little prospect for the creation of a successful democracy, chiefly by stratifying society into preferred classes. An interesting juxtaposition is Egypt. While an officially secular nation under Nasser's political ideology, Egypt was overwhelming defeated by the Israelis during the 1967 war. The resultant period of Islamic revivalism throughout the country forced his successor to return to Islam as a means of political legitimization. The loss of the 1967 war is viewed in Egypt as inextricably linked to Nasserism. The 1973 victory against Israel is viewed as a victory of and for Islam, a view that was

---

<http://www.idea.int/publications/arab_world/arabworld.pdf>. Hereafter cited as International IDEA, *Democracy*.

[102] International IDEA, *Democracy*, 9.

[103] International IDEA, *Democracy*, 9.

[104] Wright, 65.

fostered by Anwar Sadat.[105] In the current wave of Islamic revivalism mentioned above, Islam becomes a powerful and necessary legitimator for Muslim governments. Islam as a tool of legitimization likewise opens the door to Islam as a vehicle for political expression. In fact, "in the Middle East, there are a number of countries with 'brutal and all-pervasive internal security structures' that create an atmosphere conducive to Islamic opposition movements."[106] As has been shown above, political repression coupled with Islamic revivalism can create Islamic radicalism.

Heretofore, the United States has espoused democratic transition and improvement in the region. However, the current political situation should be sufficient indication that it has not met its goals. There are a number of reasons the United States meets with limited success in its efforts to export democracy and its associated institutions. The U.S. retains a great deal of influence in many parts of the Muslim world, merely because of its economic and military clout. The benefits of a close relationship with the United States are manifest to most foreign nations, at least to those people who stand to benefit from the relationship. Until now America has taken a fairly narrow approach to ideas like fostering democracy, chiefly because of the angst it causes among close friends like King Fahd of Saudi Arabia or President Mubarak of Egypt. The people repressed in the region see the relationship from a far different perspective. From their vantage point the United States maintains a double standard in its foreign policy by supporting regimes whose values are fundamentally inconsistent with its own solely for economic reasons. They make statements or ask questions such as: "...why do you

---

[105] The 1973 Arab-Israeli war was essentially fought to a tie and brought to a close through the implementation of UN Security Council Resolution 339. The idea of an Egyptian victory is based chiefly on the notion that Sadat brought to a close the period of "no peace - no war" characterized by the years intervening the '67 and '73 wars. More concretely, Egypt's ultimate reclamation of the Sinai was an outgrowth of their success in the '73 war.

[106] Deborah Gerner and Philip Schrodt, "Middle Eastern Politics," in Deborah Gerner, ed., *Understanding the Contemporary Middle East.* (Boulder: Lynne Reiner, 2000), 99.

deserve peace in Israel and the U.S. but we don't deserve peace in Iraq, Afghanistan, and Palestine?" "Why do you care about the occupation of Kuwait by Iraq but not the occupation of Palestine by Israel?" "It's shameful that the sons of Jefferson would go to a King just to get rid of the Taliban."[107]

Similarly, economic interests represented by U.S. presence in the region offend many. The view that Americans are concerned chiefly with their own economic interests does not dovetail well with concurrent American rhetoric espousing democracy. To many in the region, "...globalization has had in many respects not only a negative impact in the Arab region politically and economically, but has also deepened identity crises and threatened local values through an emphasis on consumption and market culture."[108] Some of America's allies and chief trading partners have the least democratic governments in the region. Among these are Saudi Arabia, Egypt, Jordan, Kuwait, and Pakistan.

The other major obstacle to U.S. influence in the region is that to most Arabs, America is on the wrong side of a very unjust conflict. The overwhelming view in the Muslim world is that Palestine suffers under a brutal occupation by the Israelis. This situation complicates relationships between the U.S. and regional governments as well. For example, "...in both Jordan and Egypt...public opinion on the legitimacy of the rulers [is] closely connected to acceptance (or lack thereof) of any attempts to normalize relations with Israel."[109] Concern over American support for Israel continues to fester in the

---

[107] The author heard these comments during an October 2001 National Public Radio broadcast. The guests were Arab journalists reporting for al-Jazeera and two other media outlets. The discussion was intended to provide insight into the question of Arab-U.S. relations and enmities. The statement referring to the Taliban reflected visits by U.S. Senators to Rome to meet with ousted Afghani King Zahir Shah.

[108] International IDEA, *Democracy*, 16.

[109] International IDEA, *Democracy*, 15.

Muslim world, in part because many believe the United States has the power to end the conflict, but does not do it.

One final barrier to U.S. efforts has to do with its perceptions of the preconditions for successful democracy. The view among Americans, primarily as a cultural and historical outgrowth, is that democracy and religion will not mix. The historical tradition of the separation of church and state forms the basis for this view. However, "...neither Islam nor its culture is the major obstacle to political modernity, even if undemocratic rulers sometimes use Islam as their excuse."[110] A case in point is a recent interview of Crown Prince Abdullah of Saudi Arabia by the *Washington Post*, during which he claimed that his country's commitment to Islam, in part, forms the basis for their decision not to democratize.[111] Recent U.S. interactions with the President of Turkey followed this precept. His request to visit the United States was denied because of American generalizations about adherents of political Islam. According to Geneive Abdo, "the United States makes no distinction between Erbakan, an Islamist who came to power in a free democratic election, and the Taliban..."[112] The clear impression is that American policy makers do not discriminate between radicals using religion to justify violent revolution and politicians who use religion as the basis for political ideology.

Regardless of the range of internal and external challenges, however, the United States has a compelling interest in fostering democratic transition in the region. The threats posed to the United States by radical Islamic insurgencies today can be eliminated, at

---

[110] Robin Wright, "Islam and Liberal Democracy: Two Visions of Reformation," *Journal of Democracy*, (Spring 1996): 65.

[111] Phillip Bennett and Steve Coll, "Prince Reaffirms Saudi-U.S. Alliance: Ruler Denounces Stance on Palestinians," *Washington Post*, 29 January 2002, A15.

[112] Geneive Abdo, "How Moderate Islam is Transforming Egypt," *Washington Post*, 5 November 2000, B5.

least in part, by helping Muslim nations ameliorate the trend toward radicalization. The most compelling issue for Muslim nations, at present, is to help them avoid the possibility and consequences of revolution by radical Islamic insurgencies. The seeds of change have been planted, so the question is whether in the future countries like Saudi Arabia will look more like the Ayatollah Khomeini's Iran or the Taliban's Afghanistan than Attaturk's Turkey. The answer is largely dependent on the decisions the United States makes in the near term. In the late 1970s, American failure to predict and understand the cultural transformation in Iran, particularly relative to the Shah's repressive government, has now been the source of over 20 years of strained, if not hostile, relations and untold violence associated with state-sponsored support for terrorism.[113] The United States cannot afford to let the radical forces at work today become the only forces at work for change in the region. And ultimately, no other nation or organization has the potential to influence the situation, as does the United States.

In a conversation with Dr. Akbar Ahmed of American University, a recent speaker at the FBI academy on the subject of "Islam Today," Dr. Ahmed told the author that he felt the problems contributing to the radicalization of Islam, not only reflected in the recent terrorist event of September 11, 2001, but also in a general and increasing lack of religious tolerance associated with the revivalist trend of Islam, is a problem with roots firmly planted in the Muslim world. While Americans are inclined to look within their own society for the causes of increasingly hostile relations with Muslims, Dr. Ahmed does not see the root causes of this hostility in America. He said that Muslims must fix the problem, but that the United States will be crucial in helping them to find a solution.[114]

---

[113] The allegations of state sponsorship of terrorism come from Department of State, *Patterns*, 32. Also adopted for this note is the definition of terrorism from page vi of that same document: "...premeditated, politically motivated violence perpetrated against noncombatant targets by subnational groups or clandestine agents, usually intended to influence an audience.

[114] From a conversation between the author and Dr. Akbar Ahmed on 7 February 2002 at the FBI Academy, Quantico, VA.

The conclusion is that the U.S. can offer its assistance in setting the framework for an answer, but that its roots must be found within the Muslim culture.

Despite perceptions to the contrary, Islam offers much hope for both political and democratic advancement in the Muslim world. The opposite may not be as true as once thought. In fact, according to two experts on Middle Eastern politics, "the extreme secularism of Attaturk's constitution for Turkey is not acceptable in the current environment of Islamic revivalism."[115] In light of such limited success in pursuing secular democratic models to transplant into the region, it should be viewed as essential for American policy makers to review the methods and the standards by which they intend to measure success as they go forward. Likewise, the urgency with which this effort should proceed is manifest and is predicated on the strength of and danger presented by the radical Islamic movement today. While some may argue that none of the regimes in the Middle East are as frail or as susceptible to revolution has been indicated, consideration should be given to the rapidly shifting demographics of a growing youth bulge; increasing dissatisfaction with regimes associated with declining per capita GDP; and increasing acts of terrorism as indicators of change in the region. In a recent article highlighting grave concern over the fragility of the Saudi Arabian government, Seymour Hersh claimed that the regime is "...increasingly corrupt, alienated from the country's religious rank and file, and so weakened and frightened that it has brokered its future by channeling hundreds of millions of dollars in what amounts to protection money to fundamentalist groups that wish to overthrow it."[116] For a nation as vital to the national security of the United States to be as close to radical overthrow as suggested is cause for urgent action on behalf of American policy makers.

---

[115] Gerner and Schrodt, 91.

[116] Seymour Hersh, "King's Ransom: How Vulnerable are the Saudi Royals?," *New Yorker*, 16 October 2001, 35.

In considering a new approach to assist Muslim countries to democratize, the policy maker should bear in mind the basic principles of successful democracy and evaluate their expression in ways unique to the Islamic culture. Heretofore, the United States has subscribed to its own precepts for democratic transition. According to the National Security Strategy of 2000,

> Genuine, lasting democracy...requires respect for human rights, including the right to political dissent; freedom of religion and belief; an independent media capable of engaging an informed citizenry; a robust civil society and strong Non-governmental Organization structures; the rule of law and an independent judiciary; open and competitive economic structures; mechanisms to safeguard minorities from oppressive rule by the majority; full respect for women's and workers' rights; and civilian control of the military.[117]

These views, taken as principles, do not exclude political Islam from consideration as a legitimate form of political expression. During a recent presentation at the FBI Academy in Quantico, Virginia, the president of the Pakistani American Congress, Dr. Nisar Chaudhry, offered his views on the complementary relationship of typical American and Islamic values. He said that the intersection occurs at three points: family values, quest for justice and respect for knowledge. What makes America great and powerful, he felt, are the American political expressions of the rule of law, civil liberties and individual freedoms. It was his opinion that these values should be exported.[118]

---

[117] White House, *Global Age*, 36.

[118] From comments made by Dr. Nisar Chaudhry during a presentation at the FBI academy on 7 February 2002 on the subject of "Islam Today."

The real importance of evaluating Islam's potential for democratic, political expression is the issue of cultural authenticity. The Muslim culture is extensively bound up with the development and historical success of Islam over the past 1,300 years. It's revived importance today, both as a source of cultural identity as well as a political legitimator, mandates that it be given serious consideration as a vehicle for carrying the region through the process of democratization. According to Abdulaziz Sachedina, there are three basic views of Islam in the Muslim world:

1. Islam as a religious system that provides a creed, a set of doctrines, a rite of prescriptive practices, and moral-spiritual attitudes.

2. Islam as a historical phenomenon that provides its followers with a transnational religious and national cultural identity.

3. Islam as a civilizational force that continues to shape the Muslim response to social-political realities and contingencies, allowing for necessary adjustments to membership in a diverse global community.[119]

To be successful, the policy maker's end state ought, therefore, to consider the following key elements: cultural authenticity; political legitimacy; global competitiveness measured in the context of the elements of national power; and international responsibility. The policy maker's focus should be on the indirect approach whose weapons are influence and ideas more than guns and bombs: liberal democracy (expression), free markets (opportunity and interest/participation), and rule of law (equality) coupled with a moderate expression of *Sharia* as a moral framework and the basis for interpersonal action (including the citizen's dealings with his government). As has been shown, cultural authenticity and political legitimacy are often bound together. To be legitimate, a government must represent the needs of its citizens, but also reflect

---

[119] Abdulaziz Sachedina, *The Islamic Roots of Democratic Pluralism*, (New York: Oxford University Press, 2001), 15.

their values. Among Thoreau's famous views on the subject, is the contention that

"...the government itself...is only the mode which the people have chosen to execute

their will..."[120] While this view may not obtain in the Muslim world today, infusing the

Muslim world with this idea will be essential to successful democratic transition. In the

context of the stated end state, if one accepts that economic success has the potential

for following democratic transition and a freer environment of political expression, the

question becomes: which ideas occurring naturally in the Muslim world, particularly in

Islam, will lend themselves to successful democratic transition?

---

[120] Henry David Thoreau, *Walden: On the Duty of Civil Disobedience*, (New York: Rinehart Co., Inc., 1950), 281.

Democracy in Islam

> *Let there be no compulsion in religion: Truth stands out clear from Error: whoever*
> *rejects evil and believes in God hath grasped the most trustworthy handhold, that*
> *never breaks. And God heareth and knoweth all things.*
>   *-the Qur'an (2:256)* [121]

Having recognized very little success in establishing and maintaining democratic institutions in the Muslim world to date, it seems fair to wonder why any hope exists to offer much confidence of movement in that direction. The key idea supporting the possibility of democratic transition in the region, expressed by a Tunisian named Rachid al-Ghannouchi, is that Islam defined only general principles to guide the Muslim's life and existence.[122] In other words, the body of work comprising *Sharia*, including the *Qur'an*, is man's interpretation of the implementation of those principles on earth. There are competing views and, frankly, limited consensus on a number of fundamental issues. No one has an inherent advantage in interpreting the *Qur'an*: "...the absence of the only authoritative interpreter of the message, namely the Prophet himself, precludes any claim to a definitive understanding of the Koran on the part of the community."[123] This idea should be viewed as an opportunity to policy makers who can leverage culturally relevant ideas in an effort to engender democratic transition. In fact, one expert on the subject claimed to "...firmly believe that if Muslims were made aware of the centrality of Koranic teachings about religious and cultural pluralism as a divinely ordained principle of peaceful coexistence among human societies, then they would

---

[121] The Middle East Institute, *The Religion of Islam*, URL:
<http://209.196.144.55/library/islam/religion.htm>. Accessed on 8 February 2002.
[122] Wright, 73.
[123] Sachedina, 16.

spurn violence in challenging their repressive and grossly inefficient governments."[124] Among the ideas that have relevance to this discussion are *ijma*, *ijtihad*, and *shura*.

These ideas are embedded in Islamic tradition and are indisputably, culturally authentic. *Ijma* means consensus, *ijtihad* means independent reasoning, and *shura* means consultation. "Islam teaches principles of freedom, human dignity, equality, governance by contract, popular sovereignty, and the rule of law that are compatible with but not identical to the cognate principles that belong to the intellectual heritage of liberal democracy."[125]

The idea of consultation supports the Western idea of a universal electoral process, or the fundamental basis of the democratic republic. The key behind *shura* is that "...decision making belongs to the community as a whole."[126] Despite the last hundred or so years of Muslim history, "Islamic tradition strongly disapproves of arbitrary rule."[127] Thus a ruler is compelled to review decisions with his followers. Interestingly, Muslims have a history of rejecting despots, an idea which must give pause to some authoritarians today. However, as has been suggested, a Muslim body politic fashioned along lines suggested by Islamic theology might look a bit different than those the West have come to know. For example, the idea that democratic government relies on parties representing constituencies of different views might not gain the same traction as it does in the West.[128] Further, depending on the nature of the implementation of Islamism, development of laws would likely follow *Sharia* as a constitutional basis. In

---

[124] Sachedina, 13.

[125] Laith Kubba, "Islam and Liberal Democracy: Recognizing Pluralism," *Journal of Democracy*, Spring 1996, 86.

[126] Wright, 73-74.

[127] Bernard Lewis, "Islam and Liberal Democracy: A Historical Overview," *Journal of Democracy*, Spring 1996, 55.

[128] L. Carl Brown, *Religion and State: The Muslim Approach to Politics*, (New York: Columbia University Press, 2000), 153.

the least, *Sharia* would form the moral foundation of the nation and serve as the primary body of laws.

Ideas extracted from successful Western democracy, such as "...an independent media capable of engaging an informed citizenry [and] a robust civil society;..."[129] are consistent with the idea of *ijtihad*. Historically, "all Muslims were able--indeed, were enjoined--to understand the Islamic precepts governing life in this world and to adjust their lives accordingly."[130] The fundamental premise of democracy is freedom--that one's will is enabled an opportunity for expression. Without being able to make one's own decisions regarding not only matters of faith, but also matters of government, one is not truly free. It is this tradition requiring the Muslim to critically analyze that also forms the basis of individual responsibility and accountability. Relying on Thoreau once again, "...why has every man a conscience, then? I think that we should be men first and subjects afterward."[131] The leverage that the policy maker gains is this idea of responsibility coupled with freedom. Importantly, infused within the Islamic tradition is this idea that no one has a greater opportunity to understand the Qur'an than anyone else. There are no priests who serve to interpret divine word. The individual accepts that duty. "Their empowerment is complete since Islam does not have an institution or person as a sole authority to represent the faith--or contradict their interpretations."[132]

The last basic idea mentioned is *ijma*, or consensus. Coupled with *ijtihad*, and *shura*, *ijma* most closely resembles the Western parliament. This practice is premised upon the Islamic tradition of Muslim scholars reaching conclusion on interpretation of matters

---

[129] White House, *Strategy*, 25.
[130] Brown, 97.
[131] Thoreau, 282.
[132] Wright, 73.

of law. Referring to the Qur'an, the life of the prophet and past decisions is also similar to the Western system of courts. One definition views *ijma* as:

> The adherence of the congregation of Muslims to the conclusions of a given ruling pertaining to what is permitted and what is forbidden after the passing of the Prophet...by "congregation of Muslims" [is meant] the experts of independent reasoning and legal answers in the obscure matters which require insight and investigation, as well as the agreement of the Community of Muslims concerning what is obligatorily known of the religion with its decisive proofs. [133]

This body of experts would therefore interpret, and perhaps create, laws. Recognizing the importance of *Sharia*, as a cultural requirement is critical. "...No Islamic state can be legitimate in the eyes of its subjects without obeying...*Sharia*. A secular government might coerce obedience, but Muslims will not abandon their belief that state affairs should be supervised by the just teachings of the holy law." [134]

These ideas are Muslim. That they are similar to the ideas that have sustained Western democracy for over two centuries should be reassuring to U.S. policy makers. That they come from a theological background is cause for reflection, but the moderate ideologies which have embraced and absorbed them also claim to support tolerance and inclusion. In contrast, radical Islamic ideologies do not contain ideas like fairness, equality, and individual freedom. They rely on the strictest interpretation of the Qur'an to foster the creation of a rigid and intolerant society suited only to their unique and

---

[133] Shaykh Hisham Muhammad Kabbani, *Questions on Ijma` (Consensus), Taqlid (Following Qualified Opinion), and Ikhtilaf al-Fuqha' (Differences of the Jurists)*, URL: <http://www.sunnah.org/fiqh/ijma.htm>, accessed 27 Feb 2002.

[134] Mohammed Elhachmi Hamdi, "Islam and Liberal Democracy: The Limits of the Western Model," *Journal of Democracy,* Spring 1996, 84.

narrow perspective. The radicals offer simple solutions, but no real hope for a better future.

Conclusion

The Koran...was approached as a living source of prescriptive guidance for the community. Muslim jurists sought solutions to concrete problems under given circumstances by applying the rules derived from the Koranic precedents.[135]
> -Abdulaziz Sachedina

"Muslims will continue to turn to Islam as a source of personal and communal identity and moral guidance, but they will also critically assess the legacy handed down by previous generations who may have narrowed Islam in ways that had less to do with the essence of the faith than with historical accidents and parochial circumstances."[136]

Islam is a collection of principles that have been shaped and accommodated to a myriad of cultures throughout the last 1,300 years. Today Islam is presented a threat, both internally from radicalized elements seeking radical change, and externally from a "modern world in which...Muslim states [are] situated in a non-Muslim international order."[137] And yet there are a host of moderate voices that seek change along lines that are similar to Western political evolution. The U.S. needs to give voice to the moderates; it cannot let the radicals define the nature of political Islam.

America has the opportunity today to make a dramatic impact on the future of the Muslim world. Its failure to do so thus far has been manifest in the host of terrorist attacks against it by Islamic radicals. Elimination of this radical threat will likely only be achieved through elimination of its source: corrupt, illegitimate and repressive

---

[135] Sachedina, 17.
[136] Kubba, 89.
[137] Sachedina, 13.

53

governments that, in the majority of cases, offer little hope and limited opportunity to their citizens. Reversing the trend of Muslim governments today towards expression and away from repression is no simple task, and cannot be accomplished from without. However, assistance can be provided by nations with long-standing democratic traditions if they have the wisdom to evaluate culturally authentic ideas for their intrinsically democratic value.

The roots of democracy are in Islam. *Ijma*, *ijtihad*, *shura* and *Sharia* can be parliamentary process, civil society, electoral authority and the rule of law. They are ideas with a fundamental rooting in theology, but ideas that form the cultural basis for a vast society of over one billion people. That its tradition is different from the West is clear, but that its tradition can transform has been witnessed over 1,300 years. The solution is within, but America must be prepared to assist the transition. U.S. economic interests are often served to the detriment of loftier ideals. To some, that remains the case today. According to Mohammed Elhachmi Hamdi, "what keeps all too many regimes in power in the Arab world is not their own legitimacy, but rather control over the armed forces and support from the Western nations whose interests they serve."[138] To the extent that America sustains a broken and failed system in the Muslim world, it allows radicalism to fester and revolution to foment.

---

[138] Hamdi, 84.

54

Appendices

Appendix A

Muslim Populations [139]

Countries with a Majority Muslim Population

Afghanistan: Sunni Muslim 84%, Shi'a Muslim 15%, other 1%

Albania: Muslim 70%, Albanian Orthodox 20%, Roman Catholic 10%

Algeria: Sunni Muslim (state religion) 99%, Christian and Jewish 1%

Azerbaijan: Muslim 93.4%, Russian Orthodox 2.5%, Armenian Orthodox 2.3%, other 1.8% (1995 est.)

Bahrain: Shi'a Muslim 70%, Sunni Muslim 30%

Bangladesh: Muslim 83%, Hindu 16%, other 1% (1998)

Bosnia and Herzegovina: Muslim 40%, Orthodox 31%, Roman Catholic 15%, Protestant 4%, other 10%

Brunei: Muslim (official) 67%, Buddhist 13%, Christian 10%, indigenous beliefs and other 10%

Chad: Muslim 50%, Christian 25%, indigenous beliefs (mostly animism) 25%

Cocos Islands: Sunni Muslim 57%, Christian 22%, other 21% (1981 est.)

Comoros: Sunni Muslim 98%, Roman Catholic 2%

Djibouti: Muslim 94%, Christian 6%

Egypt: Muslim (mostly Sunni) 94%, Coptic Christian and other 6%

Eritrea: Muslim, Coptic Christian, Roman Catholic, Protestant

Ethiopia: Muslim 45%-50%, Ethiopian Orthodox 35%-40%, animist 12%, other 3%-8%

Gambia, The: Muslim 90%, Christian 9%, indigenous beliefs 1%

Gaza Strip: Muslim (predominantly Sunni) 98.7%, Christian 0.7%, Jewish 0.6%

Guinea: Muslim 85%, Christian 8%, indigenous beliefs 7%

Indonesia: Muslim 88%, Protestant 5%, Roman Catholic 3%, Hindu 2%, Buddhist 1%, other 1% (1998)

Iran: Shi'a Muslim 89%, Sunni Muslim 10%, Zoroastrian, Jewish, Christian, and Baha'i 1%

---

[139] *The CIA World Factbook*, 2001.

56

Appendix A

Iraq:	Muslim 97% (Shi'a 60%-65%, Sunni 32%-37%), Christian or other 3%
Jordan:	Sunni Muslim 92%, Christian 6% (majority Greek Orthodox, but some Greek Catholics, Roman Catholics, Syrian Orthodox, Coptic Orthodox, Armenian Orthodox, and Protestant denominations), other 2% (several small Shi'a Muslim and Druze populations) (2000 est.)
Kazakhstan:	Muslim 47%, Russian Orthodox 44%, Protestant 2%, other 7%
Kuwait:	Muslim 85% (Sunni 45%, Shi'a 40%), Christian, Hindu, Parsi, and other 15%
Kyrgyzstan:	Muslim 75%, Russian Orthodox 20%, other 5%
Lebanon:	Muslim 70% (including Shi'a, Sunni, Druze, Isma'ilite, Alawite or Nusayri), Christian 30% (including Orthodox Christian, Catholic, Protestant), Jewish NEGL%
Liberia:	indigenous beliefs 40%, Christian 40%, Muslim 20%
Libya:	Sunni Muslim 97%
Malaysia:	Islam, Buddhism, Daoism, Hinduism, Christianity, Sikhism; note - in addition, Shamanism is practiced in East Malaysia
Maldives:	Sunni Muslim
Mali:	Muslim 90%, indigenous beliefs 9%, Christian 1%
Mauritania:	Muslim 100%
Mayotte:	Muslim 97%, Christian (mostly Roman Catholic)
Morocco:	Muslim 98.7%, Christian 1.1%, Jewish 0.2%
Niger:	Muslim 80%, remainder indigenous beliefs and Christians
Nigeria:	Muslim 50%, Christian 40%, indigenous beliefs 10%
Oman:	Ibadhi Muslim 75%, Sunni Muslim, Shi'a Muslim, Hindu
Pakistan:	Muslim 97% (Sunni 77%, Shi'a 20%), Christian, Hindu, and other 3%
Qatar:	Muslim 95%
Saudi Arabia:	Muslim 100%
Senegal:	Muslim 92%, indigenous beliefs 6%, Christian 2% (mostly Roman Catholic)
Sierra Leone:	Muslim 60%, indigenous beliefs 30%, Christian 10%
Somalia:	Sunni Muslim

Appendix A

Sudan:
Sunni Muslim 70% (in north), indigenous beliefs 25%, Christian 5% (mostly in south and Khartoum)

Syria:
Sunni Muslim 74%, Alawite, Druze, and other Muslim sects 16%, Christian (various sects) 10%, Jewish (tiny communities in Damascus, Al Qamishli, and Aleppo)

Tajikistan:
Sunni Muslim 80%, Shi'a Muslim 5%

Tunisia:
Muslim 98%, Christian 1%, Jewish and other 1%

Turkey:
Muslim 99.8% (mostly Sunni), other 0.2% (Christian and Jews)

Turkmenistan:
Muslim 89%, Eastern Orthodox 9%, unknown 2%

United Arab Emirates:
Muslim 96% (Shi'a 16%), Christian, Hindu, and other 4%

Uzbekistan:
Muslim 88% (mostly Sunnis), Eastern Orthodox 9%, other 3%

West Bank:
Muslim 75% (predominantly Sunni), Jewish 17%, Christian and other 8%

Western Sahara:
Muslim

Yemen:
Muslim including Shaf'i (Sunni) and Zaydi (Shi'a), small numbers of Jewish, Christian, and Hindu

Countries with a Significant Muslim Population

Cote d'Ivoire:
Christian 34%, Muslim 27%, no religion 21%, animist 15%, other 3% (1998)

Ghana:
indigenous beliefs 38%, Muslim 30%, Christian 24%, other 8%

Guinea-Bissau:
indigenous beliefs 50%, Muslim 45%, Christian 5%

Macedonia
Macedonian Orthodox 67%, Muslim 30%, other 3%

Malawi:
Protestant 55%, Roman Catholic 20%, Muslim 20%, indigenous beliefs

Mozambique:
indigenous beliefs 50%, Christian 30%, Muslim 20%

Singapore:
Buddhist (Chinese), Muslim (Malays), Christian, Hindu, Sikh, Taoist, Confucianist

Suriname:
Hindu 27.4%, Muslim 19.6%, Roman Catholic 22.8%, Protestant 25.2% (predominantly Moravian), indigenous beliefs 5%

Tanzania:
mainland - Christian 45%, Muslim 35%, indigenous beliefs 20%; Zanzibar - more than 99% Muslim

Zambia:
Christian 50%-75%, Muslim and Hindu 24%-49%, indigenous beliefs 1%

Appendix B

Per Capita Gross Domestic Product[140]

Countries with a Majority Muslim Population

Afghanistan:	$800 (2000 est.)
Albania:	$3,000 (2000 est.)
Algeria:	$5,500 (2000 est.)
Azerbaijan:	$3,000 (2000 est.)
Bahrain:	$15,900 (2000 est.)
Bangladesh:	$1,570 (2000 est.)
Bosnia andHerzegovina:	$1,700 (2000 est.)
Brunei:	$17,600 (2000 est.)
Chad:	$1,000 (2000 est.)
CocosI slands:	$NA
Comoros:	$720 (2000 est.)
Djibouti:	$1,300 (2000 est.)
Egypt:	$3,600 (2000 est.)
Eritrea:	$710 (2000 est.)
Ethiopia:	$600 (2000 est.)
Gambia, The:	$1,100 (2000 est.)
Gaza Strip:	$1,000 (2000 est.)
Guinea:	$1,300 (2000 est.)
Indonesia:	$2,900 (2000 est.)
Iran:	$6,300 (2000 est.)
Iraq:	$2,500 (2000 est.)
Jordan:	$3,500 (2000 est.)

---

[140] *The CIA World Factbook*, 2001.

Appendix B

Kazakhstan:	$5,000 (2000 est.)
Kuwait:	$15,000 (2000 est.)
Kyrgyzstan:	$2,700 (2000 est.)
Lebanon:	$5,000 (2000 est.)
Liberia:	$1,100 (2000 est.)
Libya:	$8,900 (2000 est.)
Malaysia:	$10,300 (2000 est.)
Maldives:	$2,000 (2000 est.)
Mali:	$850 (2000 est.)
Mauritania:	$2,000 (2000 est.)
Mayotte:	$600 (1998 est.)
Morocco:	$3,500 (2000 est.)
Niger:	$1,000 (2000 est.)
Nigeria:	$950 (2000 est.)
Oman:	$7,700 (2000 est.)
Pakistan:	$2,000 (2000 est.)
Qatar:	$20,300 (2000 est.)
Saudi Arabia:	$10,500 (2000 est.)
Senegal:	$1,600 (2000 est.)
Sierra Leone:	$510 (2000 est.)
Somalia:	$600 (2000 est.)
Sudan:	$1,000 (2000 est.)
Syria:	$3,100 (2000 est.)
Tajikistan:	$1,140 (2000 est.)
Tunisia:	$6,500 (2000 est.)
Turkey:	$6,800 (2000 est.)

Turkmenistan:	$4,300 (2000 est.)
United Arab Emirates:	$22,800 (2000 est.)
Uzbekistan:	$2,400 (2000 est.)
West Bank:	$1,500 (2000 est.)
Western Sahara:	$NA
World:	$7,200 (2000 est.)
Yemen:	$820 (2000 est.)

Countries with a Significant Muslim Population

Cote d'Ivoire:	$1,600 (2000 est.)
Ghana:	$1,900 (2000 est.)
Guinea-Bissau:	$850 (2000 est.)
Macedonia,	$4,400 (2000 est.)
Malawi:	$900 (2000 est.)
Mozambique:	$1,000 (2000 est.)
Singapore:	$26,500 (2000 est.)
Suriname:	$3,400 (1999 est.)
Tanzania:	$710 (2000 est.)
Zambia:	$880 (2000 est.)

Appendix C

Major Exports[141]

Countries with a Majority Muslim Population

Afghanistan: opium, fruits and nuts, handwoven carpets, wool, cotton, hides, and pelts, precious and semi-precious gems

Albania: textiles and footwear; asphalt, metals and metallic ores, crude oil; vegetables, fruits, tobacco

Algeria: petroleum, natural gas, and petroleum products 97%

Azerbaijan: oil and gas 75%, machinery, cotton, foodstuffs

Bahrain: petroleum and petroleum products 61%, aluminum 7%

Bangladesh: garments, jute and jute goods, leather, frozen fish and seafood

Bosnia and Herzegovina NA

Brunei: crude oil, natural gas, refined products

Chad: cotton, cattle, textiles

Cocos Islands: copra

Comoros: vanilla, ylang-ylang, cloves, perfume oil, copra

Djibouti: reexports, hides and skins, coffee (in transit)

Egypt: crude oil and petroleum products, cotton, textiles, metal products, chemicals

Eritrea: livestock, sorghum, textiles, food, small manufactures

Ethiopia: coffee, gold, leather products, oilseeds, qat

Gambia, The: peanuts and peanut products, fish, cotton lint, palm kernels

Gaza Strip: citrus, flowers

Guinea: bauxite, alumina, gold, diamonds, coffee, fish, agricultural products

Indonesia: oil and gas, plywood, textiles, rubber

Iran: petroleum 85%, carpets, fruits and nuts, iron and steel, chemicals

Iraq: crude oil

Jordan: phosphates, fertilizers, potash, agricultural products, manufactures

Kazakhstan: oil 40%, ferrous and nonferrous metals, machinery, chemicals, grain, wool, meat, coal

---

[141] *The CIA World Factbook*, 2001.

Appendix C

Kuwait:

oil and refined products, fertilizers

Lebanon:

foodstuffs and tobacco, textiles, chemicals, precious stones, metal and metal products, electrical equipment and products, jewelry, paper and paper products

Liberia:

diamonds, iron ore, rubber, timber, coffee, cocoa

Libya:

crude oil, refined petroleum products

Malaysia:

electronic equipment, petroleum and liquefied natural gas, chemicals, palm oil, wood and wood products, rubber, textiles

Maldives:

fish, clothing

Mali:

cotton 50%, gold, livestock (1999 est.)

Mauritania:

iron ore, fish and fish products, gold

Mayotte:

ylang-ylang (perfume essence), vanilla, copra, coconuts, coffee, cinnamon

Morocco:

phosphates and fertilizers, food and beverages, minerals

Niger:

uranium ore 65%, livestock products, cowpeas, onions (1998 est.)

Nigeria:

petroleum and petroleum products 95%, cocoa, rubber

Oman:

petroleum, reexports, fish, metals, textiles

Pakistan:

textiles (garments, cotton cloth, and yarn), rice, other agricultural products

Qatar:

petroleum products 80%, fertilizers, steel

Saudi Arabia:

petroleum and petroleum products 90%

Senegal:

fish, ground nuts (peanuts), petroleum products, phosphates, cotton

Sierra Leone:

diamonds, rutile, cocoa, coffee, fish

Somalia:

livestock, bananas, hides, fish (1999)

Sudan:

oil and petroleum products, cotton, sesame, livestock, groundnuts, gum arabic, sugar

Syria:

petroleum 65%, textiles 10%, manufactured goods 10%, fruits and vegetables 7%, raw cotton 5%, live sheep 2%, phosphates 1% (1998 est.)

Tajikistan:

aluminum, electricity, cotton, fruits, vegetable oil, textiles

Tunisia:

textiles, mechanical goods, phosphates and chemicals, agricultural products, hydrocarbons

Turkey:

apparel 25.6%, foodstuffs 15.4%, textiles 12.3%, metal manufactures

8.6%, transport equipment 8.1% (1998)

Turkmenistan: gas 33%, oil 30%, cotton fiber 18%, textiles 8% (1999)

United Arab Emirates: crude oil 45%, natural gas, reexports, dried fish, dates

Uzbekistan: cotton, gold, natural gas, mineral fertilizers, ferrous metals, textiles, food products, automobiles

West Bank: olives, fruit, vegetables, limestone

Western Sahara: phosphates 62%

World: the whole range of industrial and agricultural goods and services

Yemen: crude oil, coffee, dried and salted fish

Countries with a Significant Muslim Population

Cote d'Ivoire: cocoa 33%, coffee, tropical woods, petroleum, cotton, bananas, pineapples, palm oil, cotton, fish (1999)

Ghana: gold, cocoa, timber, tuna, bauxite, aluminum, manganese ore, diamonds

Guinea-Bissau: cashew nuts 70%, shrimp, peanuts, palm kernels, sawn lumber -1996

Macedonia   food, beverages, tobacco; miscellaneous manufactures, iron and steel

Malawi: tobacco, tea, sugar, cotton, coffee, peanuts, wood products

Mozambique: prawns 40%, cashews, cotton, sugar, citrus, timber; bulk electricity (2000)

Singapore: machinery and equipment (including electronics), chemicals, mineral fuels

Suriname: alumina, crude oil, lumber, shrimp and fish, rice, bananas

Tanzania: coffee, manufactured goods, cotton, cashew nuts, minerals, tobacco, sisal (1996)

Zambia: copper, cobalt, electricity, tobacco

Appendix D

Unemployment Rate [142]

Countries with a Majority Muslim Population

Afghanistan:	NA%
Albania:	16% (2000 est.) officially; may be as high as 25%
Algeria:	30% (1999 est.)
Azerbaijan:	20% (1999 est.)
Bahrain:	15% (1998 est.)
Bangladesh:	35.2% (1996)
Bosnia and Herzegovina:	35%-40% (1999 est.)
Brunei:	4.9% (1995 est.)
Chad:	NA%
Comoros:	20% (1996 est.)
Djibouti:	50% (2000 est.)
Egypt:	11.5% (2000 est.)
Eritrea:	NA%
Ethiopia:	NA%
Gambia, The:	NA%
Gaza Strip:	40% (includes West Bank) (yearend 2000)
Guinea:	NA%
Indonesia:	15%-20% (1998 est.)
Iran:	14% (1999 est.)
Iraq:	NA%
Jordan:	15% official rate; actual rate is 25%-30% (1999 est.)
Kazakhstan:	13.7% (1998 est.)
Kuwait:	1.8% (official 1996 est.)
Lebanon:	18% (1997 est.)

---

[142] *The CIA World Factbook*, 2001.

Appendix D

Liberia: 0.7

Libya: 30% (2000 est.)

Malaysia: 2.8% (2000 est.)

Maldives: NEGL%

Mali: NA%

Mauritania: 23% (1995 est.)

Mayotte: 45% (1997)

Morocco: 23% (1999 est.)

Niger: NA%

Nigeria: 28% (1992 est.)

Oman: NA%

Pakistan: 6% (FY99/00 est.)

Qatar: NA%

Saudi Arabia: NA%

Senegal: NA%; urban youth 40%

Sierra Leone: NA%

Somalia: NA%

Sudan: 4% (1996 est.)

Syria: 20% (2000 est.)

Tajikistan: 5.7% includes only officially registered unemployed; also large numbers of underemployed workers and unregistered unemployed people (December 1998)

Tunisia: 15.6% (2000 est.)

Turkey: 5.6% (plus underemployment of 5.6%) (2000 est.)

Turkmenistan: NA%

United Arab Emirates: NA%

Uzbekistan: 10% plus another 20% underemployed (1999 est.)

Appendix D

West Bank:	40% (includes Gaza Strip) (yearend 2000)
Western Sahara:	NA%
World:	30% combined unemployment and underemployment in many non-industrialized countries; developed countries typically 4%-12% unemployment (2000 est.)
Yemen:	30% (1995 est.)

Countries with a Significant Muslim Population

Cote d'Ivoire:	13% in urban areas (1998 est.)
Ghana:	20% (1997 est.)
Guinea-Bissau:	NA%
Macedonia	32% (2000)
Malawi:	NA%
Mozambique:	21% (1997 est.)
Singapore:	3% (2000 est.)
Suriname:	20% (1997)
Tanzania:	NA%
Zambia:	50% (2000 est.)

www.ingramcontent.com/pod-product-compliance
Lightning Source LLC
Chambersburg PA
CBHW080533290526
45790CB00006B/2384